Brooklyn Bridge

ABDO
Publishing Company

A Buddy Book
by
Sarah Tieck

VISIT US AT
www.abdopublishing.com

Published by ABDO Publishing Company, 8000 West 78th Street, Edina, Minnesota 55439.

Printed in the United States.

Contributing Editor: Michael P. Goecke
Graphic Design: Deborah Coldiron
Cover Photograph: Photos.com
Interior Photographs/Illustrations: Library of Congress (pages 5, 7, 9, 12, 18, 19, 20, 21); Photos.com (pages 6, 10, 11, 13, 15, 16, 17, 22)

Library of Congress Cataloging-in-Publication Data

Tieck, Sarah, 1976-
    Brooklyn Bridge / Sarah Tieck.
        p. cm. — (All aboard America)
    Includes index.
    ISBN 978-1-59928-934-2
    1. Brooklyn Bridge (New York, N.Y.)—History—Juvenile literature. 2. New York
(N.Y.)—Buildings, structures, etc.—Juvenile literature. I. Title.

    TG25.N53T54 2008
    624.2'3097471—dc22

                                                                2007027263

Table of Contents

An Important Bridge 4

Sharing A Vision 6

A Strong Design 8

A Bridge Of Firsts 12

Building Challenges 16

The Brooklyn Bridge Today 22

Important Words 23

Web Sites 23

Index 24

CHAPTER 1

An Important Bridge

The Brooklyn Bridge is one of the most important bridges ever constructed.

At first, people said it couldn't be built. When it was finished, it was the world's longest suspension bridge! It was also the strongest. People called it an engineering **achievement**.

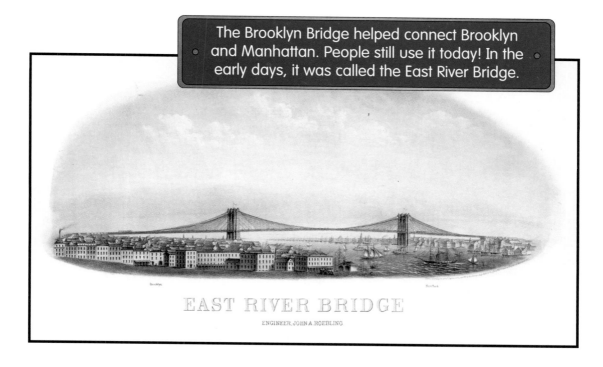

The Brooklyn Bridge helped connect Brooklyn and Manhattan. People still use it today! In the early days, it was called the East River Bridge.

EAST RIVER BRIDGE

ENGINEER, JOHN A. ROEBLING

The Brooklyn Bridge met a great need for New York City, New York. And, it helped the city grow and gain importance.

At one time, the only way to get from Manhattan to Brooklyn was by boat. The East River was about one-third of a mile (.5 km) wide. There was a lot of wind and many boats on the river. Travel was very slow, especially in winter.

John Roebling

An engineer named John Roebling had an idea for a bridge. Many people didn't think his plan would work. Still, Roebling **designed** a strong bridge for the river.

It took many years for Roebling to get approval to build his bridge. The East River was very powerful. People weren't sure Roebling's bridge would be strong enough.

AMERICAN VIEWS.

NEW YORK CITY.

Workers broke ground on January 3, 1870. It took more than five years to complete the two towers.

CHAPTER 3

A Strong Design

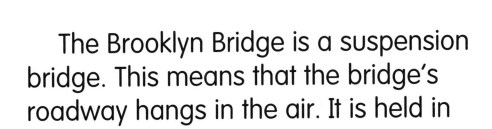

The Brooklyn Bridge is a suspension bridge. This means that the bridge's roadway hangs in the air. It is held in place by towers and cables.

The first step in building the bridge's two towers was to lay **foundations**. Workers did this in dangerous caissons. These wooden boxes rested on the river bottom. They were filled with air and did not let in water. But inside caissons it was hot and **humid**.

Workers climbed ladders down into the caissons. As the towers grew, the caissons sank to a layer of **bedrock**. These made a strong **foundation** for the 25-story-tall towers!

About 100 workers were in the caissons at one time. Candles provided light.

The 25-story towers were built on top of strong foundations deep underwater.

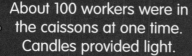

Strong steel cables are another important part of the bridge. Four main cables hang from the top of the bridge. Each one is 16 inches (41 cm) thick!

Bundling the Main Cables

Securing the Anchorages

Workers built anchorages. These held the ends of the main cables in place. The anchorages weighed 120 million pounds (54 million kg).

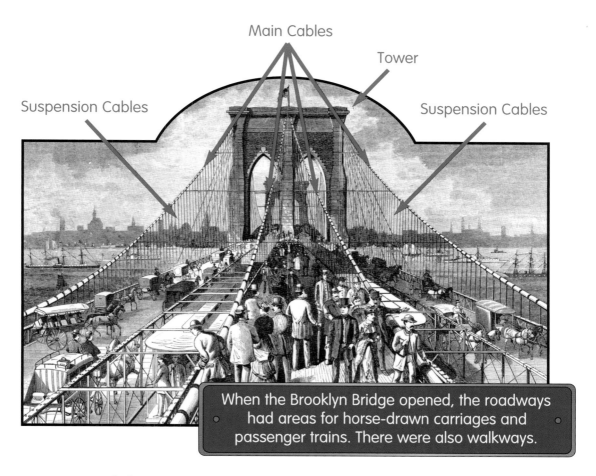

Main Cables

Tower

Suspension Cables

Suspension Cables

When the Brooklyn Bridge opened, the roadways had areas for horse-drawn carriages and passenger trains. There were also walkways.

Roebling engineered the bridge to be very safe and strong. About 1,500 steel suspension cables hang from the main cables. These hold the roadways and walkways.

CHAPTER 4

A Bridge Of Firsts

The Brooklyn Bridge opened on May 24, 1883. People were very proud and excited. The new bridge had shown that many things were possible.

While digging the **foundation**, workers found a layer of boulders. To break through, they used explosives in the caissons. This was a first!

The bridge opened to walkers around 2 PM and to other traffic at 5 PM. The evening ended with fireworks.

Workers created the steel cables used in the Brooklyn Bridge.

The Roeblings owned a company that made steel wire. They used their wire to make cables for the bridge. The Brooklyn Bridge was the first suspension bridge to use steel cables.

And at the time it was built, the Brooklyn Bridge held a very special record. It was the longest suspension bridge in the world!

Detour ▼

Fun Facts

- The total cost of the Brooklyn Bridge was about $15 million.

- The official length of the bridge is 6,016 feet (1,834 m). This is a little longer than one mile!

- Workers were paid just $2 per day!

- The Brooklyn Tower rests at about 44 feet (13 m) below the surface. The New York Tower's foundation is almost 80 feet (24 m) beneath the surface.

• **The longest part of the bridge supported just by cables is about 1,600 feet (490 m)!**

• **In 1984, a bike lane was added to the bridge.**

There used to be a charge to cross the bridge. It cost five cents to drive and three cents to walk. Today, it is free.

It took 13 years to build the Brooklyn Bridge. It was very dangerous. Fires, explosions, and other construction accidents killed about 30 people.

Before construction started, Roebling was hurt in an accident. He died and his son, Washington, took over.

Washington Roebling

The bridge's towers are made from granite. Workers used dangerous caissons in constructing the towers.

In 1872, Washington Roebling was **paralyzed** by caisson disease. He worked from home with his wife, Emily, who helped him finish the bridge.

Many other workers got very sick from the same illness during construction. The **compressed air** in the caissons caused a lot of body pain.

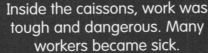
Inside the caissons, work was tough and dangerous. Many workers became sick.

Detour ▼

Did You Know?

Emily Warren Roebling made sure the bridge was constructed. She learned about engineering and visited the site each day. She often delivered messages from Washington Roebling, who watched from his bedroom.

Emily Roebling

Detour ▼

Did You Know?

. . . Washington Roebling watched the opening of the bridge from his apartment. He never visited the site after he got sick.

. . . To show the bridge's strength, P.T. Barnum walked 21 circus elephants across it in 1884!

P.T. Barnum

. . . The Brooklyn Bridge was painted "Rawlins Red." This color came from a mine in Rawlins, Wyoming.

. . . Until 1944, people could take elevated trains across the bridge. And until 1950, people could ride streetcars over the bridge.

. . . In 1878, people were allowed to cross a footbridge between the towers. It was very high!

Many workers used the wooden footbridge to move around the work site.

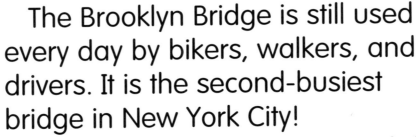
The Brooklyn Bridge Today

The Brooklyn Bridge is still used every day by bikers, walkers, and drivers. It is the second-busiest bridge in New York City!

It remains a favorite **landmark** for Americans. And, it is still considered an important **achievement** in the engineering world.

Today, about 144,000 cars cross the Brooklyn Bridge each day.

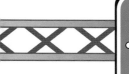

Important Words

achievement something done successfully using skill, work, or courage.

bedrock a solid layer of rock beneath rocks, gravel, and soil.

compressed air air that is under pressure.

design making a plan to create something.

foundation the base that helps to support a building structure.

humid air that is warm and damp.

landmark a feature that is easily recognized.

paralyzed being unable to move one's body.

WEB SITES

To learn more about the Brooklyn Bridge, visit ABDO Publishing Company on the World Wide Web. Web sites about the Brooklyn Bridge are featured on our Book Links page. These links are routinely monitored and updated to provide the most current information available.

www.abdopublishing.com

Index

anchorages **10**

Barnum, P.T. **20**

Brooklyn **5, 6**

caisson disease **18**

caissons **8, 9, 12, 18**

East River **5, 6, 7, 8**

engineer **4, 6, 11, 19, 22**

foundation **8, 9, 12, 14**

granite **17**

Manhattan **5, 6**

New York City, New York **5, 22**

Rawlins, Wyoming **21**

Roebling, Emily Warren **18, 19**

Roebling, John **6, 7, 11, 13, 16**

Roebling, Washington **16, 18, 19, 20**

steel **10, 11, 13**

suspension cables **8, 10, 11, 13, 15**

towers **7, 8, 9, 11, 17, 21**

workers **7, 8, 9, 10, 12, 14, 18, 21**